The
Harting
Training
System

by
Dr. Marcella Vonn Harting, Ph.D.

The Harting Training System

To order more copies of this book, use the order form on the last page of this book or visit www.MarcellaVonnHarting.com

Marcella Vonn Harting, PhD
8714 N 58th Place
Paradise Valley AZ 85253
(480) 443-3224 phone
(480) 443-0302 fax

Printed and bound in the United States of America

Table of Contents

Acknowledgements

From the deepest part of my being, I express my heart-felt love and gratitude to my husband, Jim, who has contributed encouragement, support and love in me following my dreams and aspirations.

To my dear friend, Donald Clair, for his brilliant wisdom and loving support with the birth of this book.

To all the people in my organization for their drive and constant search to better their health for themselves and others.

About the Author

Marcella Vonn Harting, PhD is an internationally recognized author, speaker, facilitator and entrepreneur. Involved with Network MultiLevel Marketing since the 1980's, Marcella Vonn has built two highly successful businesses with more than 1,000,000 representatives worldwide. In her Leadership Playshops she demonstrates how creating a residual abundant income centered in health and wealth can empower balance and purpose in one's life.

Marcella Vonn has lectured throughout the United States, Canada, Europe, Australia, Japan, Mexico, Singapore, and Malaysia. She combines nutrition, conscious communications, face and body language into her dynamic presentations to assist people in creating the life of their heart's desires and dreams.

With certifications in Nutrition, Iridology, Reiki, International Aromatherapy through PIA, Master Practitioner of Neuro-Linguistic Programming, Master Practitioner of Hypnotherapy, PhD in Psychoneurology & Integrated Health, Anthony Robbins Digital Delivery Event Leader and as a Personal Trainer, Marcella Vonn is an inspirational mentor and coach in manifesting and teaching how to achieve one's divine purpose with grace and ease and fun.

Marcella Vonn has co-authored several books including

"Yes, No, Maybe" Chronobiotic Nutrition with G.I. Atom Bergstrom and the book *Guerrilla Multilevel Marketing* with Jay Conrad Levinson and James Dillehay, and has been featured on CNN. She has also authored *The Harting Training System Book* and *Aromatic Essential Cards.* She is co-author of *Prosperity Factor* with Dr. Joe Vitale and *The Women's Millionaire Club* with Maureen G. Mulvaney, MGM.

In Network Marketing she demonstrates how creating a residual abundant income centered in health and wealth can empower balance and purpose in one's life. Marcella Vonn is an inspirational mentor in manifesting and teaching how to achieve one's divine purpose with grace and ease and fun.

Marcella Vonn Harting has achieved the rank of Royal Crown Diamond in Young Living Essential Oils. This is a monumental achievement because the Royal Crown Diamond rank is the highest level that a distributor can succeed to in Young Living's compensation plan.

Married since 1980 and the mother of two children, she resides in Paradise Valley, Arizona.

About the Publisher

James Dillehay, a Diamond level network marketer is author of 8 books, a marketing coach, and seminar leader. He is a nationally recognized expert on helping people with big dreams and small budgets generate income streams successfully. James' books and articles have been recommended by *The Chicago Tribune, Family Circle, Working Mothers, Country Almanac* and many more. He has been listed in *Who's Who of American Entrepreneurs.* He is co-author with Marcella Vonn Harting and Jay Conrad Levinson of the book, *Guerrilla Multilevel Marketing.*

About the Writer

Lorie Ann Buchanan has been journaling since age 8, and won her first writing contest at age 10. Self-employed for almost 20 years, she specializes in health services of the home environment as a Professional Organizer and of the human environment as a Reiki Master, Personal Fitness Trainer and network marketing professional. She is on the Spiritual Leadership Council at her "home base" church in Walla Walla, Washington and alternately resides in Washington, Oregon and Arizona. She is looking forward to traveling more with her husband and publishing more of her writings. Her greatest joy is movement, whether it is dancing, running, riding, or helping others move towards their goals and aspirations.

About the Editor

Cathy Marley is an award-winning author and owner of CJM Communications, Inc. where she helps small businesses succeed through ghost and contract writing, editing, marketing and media relations. With projects as varied as her clientele, she has written and edited news releases and corporate and independent newsletters, authored fundraising communications for the arts community and developed marketing and publicity materials. She has been published in a variety of national and local publications and edited Marcella Vonn Harting's first book, *"Yes, No, Maybe" Chronobiotic Nutrition* as well as the soon-to-be-released creative memoir *When Irish Eyes are Lying* by Joy Malumphy. An author in her own right, she published her first book, *Peeking Over the Edge…views from life's middle*, a heartfelt collection of personal reflections exploring self image, self awareness, love, connection to the world and the legacy we create, in 2006. She also has a significant presence in *Love in Bloom*, a collection of love stories written by the Women Writers of the Desert. Cathy lives in Phoenix, Arizona with her husband Norm and can be reached at www.CathyMarley.com.

Introduction

This book is designed as a tool for you to create success. It is designed to teach you how to be successful even faster than I have been. So before you read any further, ask yourself two questions: "Am I teachable? Or "Do I already know it all?" If you are teachable, keep reading. Use this book diligently, and use it as it is written. Do what I tell you to do, exactly as I tell you to do it, without any excuses.

I am Marcella Vonn Harting. I have been married to my husband, Jim, since 1980, and we live in Paradise Valley, Arizona with our two Bulldogs. We have a daughter, Kortni, and a son, Dallas. I have traveled the world teaching and I am committed to sharing my passion for empowering people.

When my little girl was born she had swallowed meconium, the tar-like bowel movement of infants and it poisoned her system. At seven months old my daughter had a severe case of pneumonia and she literally died in my husband's arms as we rushed to the hospital. God miraculously gave her back to us. We lived in the critical care unit of the hospital for ten days. When my daughter was three, a team of doctors told me she was retarded and nothing could be done for her. I refused to accept their diagnosis. I started investigating alternative health and nutrition. If someone said they had something to help my daughter, I was right there checking it out.

My husband and I were overjoyed as we saw significant positive changes in her abilities from investigating products and resources from a network marketing company. The changes were so substantial, her teachers and the parents of her friends started asking me what I was doing. It was amazing to watch my daughter's progress. She went from being diagnosed as retarded to graduating from college with a degree. During those years I was so focused on helping people feel better, I wasn't interested in making money. It wasn't until my check started getting big I even realized I had a business. I had been plugging away through all sorts of company changes, hanging in there like a bulldog, until one day I looked at my five figure commission check and I realized I had a successful business. I felt such a strong gratitude and moral responsibility to support the people in my organization, I sat down and cried. The reason I did this was not the company, or the products or the money; it was the people! And *the* reason for my success *is* my relationships with people. My relationships have taken me to the top in my company. The level of success relies on dedication and skill level. If you would like to learn how to successfully sell, get another book. If you would like to create life-long happiness and success, get to know PEOPLE, including yourself. My Harting Training System and the Highest Potential Academy System will teach you the skills you need to travel the road of success.

The Eagle

"Watch your thoughts, for they become words.
Choose your words, for they become actions.
Understand your actions for they become your habits.
Study your habits for they will become your character.
Develop your character for it becomes your destiny."

~ Author Unknown ~

Who are you?
Are you the person you would like to be?

Once upon a time, in a kingdom that probably never really existed, people tell a story you would never believe…so don't pay full attention when I tell you this tale, and don't give it a second thought since it does not relate to you after all…

The eagle circled majestically. Her all-seeing eyes thoroughly scanned the ground below her as she soared happily along. Flying at an almost dizzying height, she imagined what it would be like to have her friends flying along beside her. She knew any eagle would love the breath-taking scenery and exhilarating flight and so she kept asking friends to come along. She had been inviting other eagles to join her on her adventures for years now, even though the responses she got were typically the same. Some would flat out say no, rejecting her heart-felt request to join her on a spectacular flight. Others would cheerfully say, "Sure I'll come along" and go as far as setting up a time and day for the flight without ever showing up. She found she preferred the direct approach over the less straight-forward deception.

Tilting her powerful wings, she used their strength to capture more wind and gain more altitude. She thought about the times when she did meet eagles excited about the possibilities of flying. It seemed to last only a certain amount of time before they became apathetic or lost interest. And then they would fly with her less and eventually stop flying with her at all. After many different variations and combinations of excuses she figured she had heard it all. She found it fascinating how creative eagles could be to get out of flying to new heights and to avoid learning new flight patterns. Some of them claimed they didn't have time to learn what she could teach them, they needed to scout for food; some elaborated about how they were too old to learn new tricks, or not old enough yet to have lessons; some claimed even though they had wings they didn't really have a talent for "high" flying or "power" flying; still others asserted they needed a group to learn in or if they were in a group, they needed a one-on-one… and on and on and on.

Well, she reflected, as she glided gracefully along towards her destination, eagles are eagles. She had invested a lot of time searching behind the different words eagles said and the different stories she heard, to find every eagle is the same at the core of their being. Change the color, change the size, change the age or change the gender, the bottom line remains the same: eagles are eagles. Every eagle has the same two barriers to successful flight: they fear they will not be loved and they believe they are not worthy.

When she acknowledged her own fears and chose to overcome them, she had a profound shift in her flying. She found she could fly further, faster and higher. She continued to fly forward with ease, the path of her flight emerging effortlessly from the power and span of her wings. She repeatedly offered to teach the other eagles how to fly as she did, to get more out of their own wings, but she was jeered at and mocked. "You can only fly to those heights because you have been flying so long and do it so often!" Really it was more the selectiveness of her lifestyle and her conscious choice in peers than the length of time or frequency of her flying contributing to her success. She surrounded herself with supportive eagles, took good care of herself, chose what thoughts she allowed herself to focus on, and a few other tricks.

Over time she had discovered similarities among the eagles who did show up to learn from her: either they gave her excuses, they wouldn't do as she told them, they only wanted to give their opinion, or they skipped the training. Some were teachable, others were know-it-alls. Upon further delving, she discovered every eagle has the same basic needs. Every eagle has needs for security, variety, love, recognition, growth, contribution and a compelling future.

Immersed in the enjoyment of her flight, her thoughts flitted through the past, when she was scoffed at by derisive others saying, "No one can fly as high as you say is possible," completely discounting her experience. She let those words go, knowing if she focused on them she would start believing them. As she abruptly changed her flight pattern to soar upward, she recalled a recent conversation with one of her peers. Her friend queried, "How can you keep inviting eagles to fly when you have had so many turn you down and let you down?" The eagle smiled to herself when she recalled the startled look on the other eagle's face when she replied, "I realize some eagles will fly, some eagles won't, so…next! I just stay in my heart and fly every day." She let it be a game to her.

As she regained her momentum, she focused single-mindedly on the enjoyment of her movement. She found vitality and a motivating force in sharing her expertise to empower other eagles. She rapidly descended creating a pleasing rush of wind against her feathers as the ground below her neared. She had visualized, felt it as so, prepared and anticipated and now she was ready to lead a new group. She reveled in the vast expanse of air she was diving through, and soared and swooped once more before sharply landing in front of the murmuring eagles gathered in an expectant group…

Network Marketing

"Richest people in the world build networks...
everyone else in the world looks for work!"

~ Robert Kiyosaki, Millionaire, Author, Coach ~

What Network Marketing is: a business in which rewards are in direct proportion to the value and effort you put forth. Network Marketing rewards you for helping others. As a definition, it could be said Network Marketing is any method of distribution allowing independent distributors to recruit other distributors and to draw a commission from the sales of these other recruits. (It is also interchangeably called Multilevel Marketing (MLM) or Direct Sales Marketing.) In Network Marketing, your downline (all the people you have recruited and your recruits have recruited and so on) grows in geometric progression, as well as your income.

The Benefits of Network Marketing: FREEDOM!

Network Marketing provides you the freedom to choose:
• You choose the who, what, when, where and how of work.
• You choose with whom you work—friends, associations, or organizations, whether one-on-one, in small gatherings or large groups.
• You choose what products and/or services you will represent and from which company, your income level, your bonuses.
• You choose when you work—what days, every day or

every other day, what hours, at night or in the morning, even while traveling.

• You choose where you work—what city, what state, at home, in an office, while in a car, on a bus or in a train.

• You choose how you work—slow advancement, part-time, rapid advancement, full-time, in person, through mailers, meetings, phone calls or Internet.

• Your business can be developed anywhere, with anyone, in one location or multiple.

• Your business can be developed in the style and manner you choose, to enhance your life and allow you to actualize your dreams and goals.

A Network Marketing company is only as strong as the power of its distributors. Weaknesses which have been attributed to the structure of Network Marketing actually appear because of character challenges within the individual distributors. The structure of Network Marketing is designed to empower, nourish and support people (distributors) sharing their belief in the positive results of a product or service. In order for a distributor to be highly successful, personal growth is the most crucial aspect of effective Network Marketing. It is the one thing separating average results from extraordinary.

How to Get Started

"The highest achievable level of service comes from the heart, so the company that reaches people's hearts will provide the best level of service."

~ Hal Rosenbluth ~

Master having a sincere interest in other people and their lives. Build rapport, get people to talk about themselves, and keep the conversation about them. Your goal is to make new life-long friends, and to meet with them again and again for their highest good and yours!

Everyone has areas of their life they would like to improve, and if you listen well, people are always telling you what they would like more of in their life. By asking specific questions, the direction of the conversation is controlled, and it is possible to elicit information. Use your "Building Block of Relationship Rapport" chapter!

Discover three important things:

1. Their needs
2. Their strengths
3. Their goals

Ask questions using the F.O.R.M.

Listen to connect their world with yours. When you find a similarity, use it to create rapport and find solutions for their life.

The "FORM" formula for success:

F = Family
   Married? Kids? School? Animals? Where do you live?

O = Occupation
   Where do you work? For whom? Like or dislike it? How long? What would you like to do?

R = Recreation
   What do you do for fun? Vacation? Time to do it? With whom?

M = Meet their needs
   What they would choose, how to meet their needs best.

Get Started

- Get on autoship.
- Use the product so you know from experience what you like about it.
- Go through your distributor/enrollment kit. Know how to enroll someone on paper, by telephone and on Internet.
- Make your resource list of 100 people you know. (Remember, no judging! The people you think will be most interested will not be, and the people you think will not be interested, will be! And they know other people who might be interested.)
  Family — (Step-)Mom, (Step-)Dad, (Step-)Sisters, (Step-)Brothers, Aunts, Uncles, Cousins, In-laws
  Friends — Co-Workers, Neighbors
  Organizations — Church, Lodges, Schools/College

Occupation and Education — Community Groups, Health, Political
Athletic contact — Fitness Center, Bowling leagues, Bicycling, Camping, Hiking, Martial Arts
People you do business with — Banking, Health, Beauty, Sales, Transportation, Construction, Medical, Dental, School contacts, Hotel, Restaurants, Travel
Holiday friends — Birthday list, Christmas list

• Go to all your company trainings – as well as other personal growth seminars. This includes Leadership Playshops. Be teachable…be open to new experiences.

Be a Product of the Product

• Develop a testimonial based on experience.
• Learn to give a great testimonial – from the heart, in the first person.
• "Facts tell, stories sell."
• Keep it simple and to the point.

Duplicate Yourself

One of the best ways you can mentor yourself is to get leadership tools into someone's hands; know your resources. (See the resource section in the back of this book.)

Communication Log

Keep records of conversations (with corporate, leads, etc.) to whom you talked, about what, and when. We are dealing with people and because we are human sometimes there are misunderstandings. A communication log is a historical record which can also be used to document rapport notes: V.A.K., Love Language, best time to call, etc.

MARCELLA VONN'S 5 SUCCESS TOOLS

1. Enthusiasm
2. Persistence
3. Gift to act (instead of react)
4. Adventure (child-like)
5. Desire (destiny is success)

Other Qualities for Success:

- Motivated
- Self-starters
- Goal-oriented
- Positive
- Credible
- Teachable
- Willing
- Follow-up
- Follow-through
- Health conscious
- Service oriented

NOW STEP UP TO THE NEXT LEVEL!

"Many hands, hearts and minds generally contribute to anyone's notable achievements."

~ Walt Disney ~

FORMULA FOR SUCCESS

80% Prospecting/Recruiting
19% Training
1% Problem-Solving
Market and Promote is your main focus!

MEETINGS

"People are like a storage battery, constantly discharging energy and unless they are recharged at frequent intervals they soon run dry."

~ Anonymous ~

RULES FOR MEETINGS

Preparation tips:
- Arrive early
- Dress professionally
- Have your room set up with support tools:
  √ product table with samples and hand-outs
  √ sign-in sheet (tax record)
- Meet your guests at the door
- Start on time

During the meeting:
- Be sincere, enthusiastic and from your heart! "It's not what you say, it's how you make them feel."
- Welcome everyone with a smile, and introduce yourself. Talk briefly about your experiences with your opportunity.
- At a home meeting, allow people to introduce themselves and briefly share their personal product experiences.

- Present company profile or give an overview.
- Present main content of presentation:
    - o Introduce guests, speakers, etc.
    - o Use support tools and products for visual, auditory and kinesthetic
    - o Edify each other (Defined as: to build up or strengthen, especially morally or spiritually.) NOTE: if you can't say something sincere, find something!
    - o Testimonies for product and business (Again: facts will tell, stories sell!)
    - o Get everyone involved, engaged and relating
- Close with opportunity to join our organization
- End on time with a smile! … and a hug or handshake for those kinesthetic people!

SOCIAL MEDIA

MEDIA (definition): the means of communication that reach large numbers of people, such as television, newspapers, and radio.

SOCIAL MEDIA: includes web-based and mobile technologies used to turn communication into interactive dialogue.

"We don't have a choice on whether we do social media the question is how well we do it."

~ Erik Qualman ~

One of the most powerful, business tools available to us is the internet. Today there are over 2.5 billion users on the web, creating a way to talk to anyone anywhere in the world. Network Marketing is all about building relationships, a business of connecting. The more we can connect, developing solid, deep, credible relationships adding value and being of service the more success you will have. This is a business more about giving than getting!

> "People do not care how much you know
> until they know how much you care."
>
> ~ John C. Maxwell ~

⌐⫰⌐

I once heard that 90% of success in life comes from showing up! With social media we can show up on professional groups like LinkedIn, Google+, Facebook, Twitter, ect, In networking, you are your product and your reputation becomes your brand, so never post anything publicly you would not want your grandmother to see! (Never do anything online or offline that will cause people to question your integrity.) The emphasis is to build genuine relationships with the smart use of technology.

In all the books I read on social media, how and why to use it with my business. I have found a few reasons using social media benefits me. I can research a new or potential customer, distributor/member and learn about them. I can learn more about the groups of the people I know and who they are connected to. I can position myself as an expert or professional. And I can use search engine optimization to make it easier for people to find me.

MARCELLA VONN'S
TOOL BOX FOR SUCCESS

√ Business building books (*Guerilla Multilevel Marketing*)
√ Brochures

√ Business cards
√ Catalog
√ DVDs / CDs
√ Enrollment form
√ Samples
√ Success kits
√ V.A.K. Sheet

CARE AND FOLLOW-UP

• Smile, smile, smile! Smile at people, smile with people, smile on the phone!
• Treat people as you would like to be treated. Be kind; deluge them with courtesy.
• Send thank-you notes within 24-48 hours.
• Have them call when get distributor/member enrollment package/kit and schedule appointment to meet on the phone, by Internet or in person.
• Have them write their goals down and share them, find out their V.A.K., Love Languages, and Seven Human Needs to use as leverage with them to achieve their goals. Wanna make a little or a lot?
• Schedule a time to meet and create a plan to achieve goals.

SUCCESS HABITS

"We are creatures of habit, change
our habits and we change our life!"

~ Marcella Vonn ~

Apply yourself. Apply and use the products. Study and learn.

Believe in people. Believe you make a difference.

Care about and **Communicate** with others—upline, downline, team, organization, cold lead, warm market, hot market…

Discipline yourself to attain your goals.

Envision your life in positive vivid detail and take action!

How to Work With Family and Really Close Friends

"Love doesn't hurt, expectations do."

~ Pushkaraj Shirke ~

W hy in this industry do the majority of people enjoyed more success from working with strangers and acquaintances than their family and the ones the love the most?

I have found with over 30 years experience in this industry the most hurt and pain people experience comes from working closely with family and friends. And it all comes down to one secret to how to work with them with success.

If I were to give you a gift and you did not accept it, what would happen to the gift?

The gift would come back to me!

Think about this for a moment. We love and care for our family and very close friends, and we want the best for them, we want to have them enjoy the lifestyle, abundance, products and benefits that we are enjoying thru this business. Right?

Our EXPECTATIONS, of what they do with this opportunity or products -use or not use. Is why we feel the hurt and pain? If you can give them the gift and have no expectations of what they do with it, then it is truly a gift and everyone can benefit.

"When you release expectations, you are free to enjoy things for what they are instead of what you think they should be."

~ Mandy Hale ~

Determine Where You Are Right Now

"There are two kinds of people who will never get ahead in life: One is the person who will not do anything more than he is told and the other is the person who will not do what he is told."

~ Anonymous ~

If I can do this, you can do this. If you are willing to do what I did, you will get the results I got. Network Marketing is a job and like any job, you have to put in the time and effort to learn to do it well and efficiently. Remember when you started the first day on a job? Remember being nervous and afraid you might not do it right? Then you were fully immersed in it for 8 hours a day, 5 days a week, and you got pretty good at it. Or remember when you had your first baby? Remember being scared about the whole experience? But you got through it and the second one was easier - you were more confident because you had some experience and more skill. A Network Marketing business is the same way. You have to put in the time and get the training to raise your skill level. The market place pays for value and what determines your value is your skill level. And YOU are in charge of this one variable.

In the formation of Network Marketing success, the base level of skill is basic fundamentals: knowing the company and its philosophy, mission/purpose, products and compensation plans. The middle level of skill is people skills: having a *sincere* interest in them (using the F.O.R.M.*), creating rapport (using the V.A.K.*), matching and mirroring, connecting with their love language. The highest level of skill is personal growth: knowing yourself and finding areas to improve and better yourself.

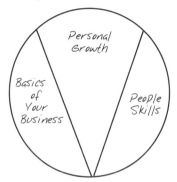

The skill level of personal growth is a key area for increasing your success. Millionaires say 95 percent of success is determined by personal growth. And guess what…the majority of the world's wealth is held by about five percent of the population! In order to go to a higher level of success, you must be willing to learn, to work and to take action! Continually evaluate yourself, train yourself, model yourself after success.

> "Life isn't about finding yourself,
> life is about creating yourself."
>
> ~ Anonymous ~

Modeling is about behavior patterns. People pick up behavior patterns consciously and unconsciously. They are often unconsciously embodied from frequent, close associations, such as the influence of parents and peers. Or they may be embodied in a more conscious manner. Think of the influence of celebrities and the people who attempt to emulate "the stars." Thank God for Oprah!!!

I am going to tell you right now, consciously choosing a successful model to emulate is what will make all the difference in your life. It is what I have done and why I have created Highest Potential Academy for you to attend. The Highest Potential Academy immerses you in an environment in which you can embody success with visual, auditory and kinesthetic experience.

Using the assessments provided below, take an honest inventory of where you are now.

✍ *Where is your skill level with the basic fundamentals?*

> "The will to succeed is important, but what's even more important is the will to prepare."
>
> ~ Bobby Knight ~

- Do you know who founded the company and why?
- Do you know the company's mission and purpose?
- Do you know the product line, how to use the products, who would benefit from them and their prices?
- Do you know the compensation plan and the levels for bonuses, if there are incentives and when they pay-out?

✍ *Where is your skill level with people?*

> "Kindness is a language we can all speak. Even the deaf can hear it and the blind can see it."
>
> ~ Mother Teresa ~

- Do people hear, see and feel your sincere interest in them?
- Do you create rapport immediately and comfortably?
- Do you know how to match and mirror effectively?
- Do look for ways to connect naturally by praise, touch or service?

✍ *Where is your level of skill in personal growth?*

"Income rarely exceeds personal development."

~ Jim Rohn ~

- Do you recognize in which areas you are complacent and find new challenges?
- Do you step outside your comfort zone to increase your capabilities?

On the Wheel of Life, what is your level of satisfaction in each area of your life? The center as 1 (lowest) and the outer edges as 10 (highest). Shade each segment according to level of satisfaction. If this were a real wheel, how bumpy would the ride be?

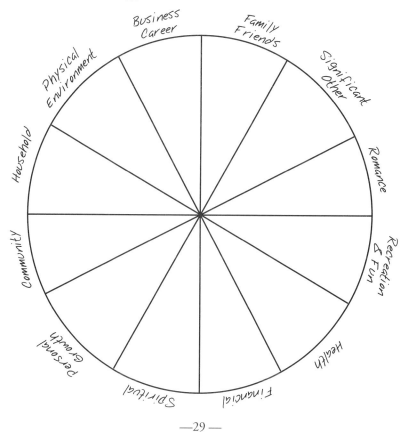

✑ On the Business Wheel of Performance, what are your levels of results? The center as 1 (lowest) and the outer edges as 10 (highest). Shade each segment according to your results.

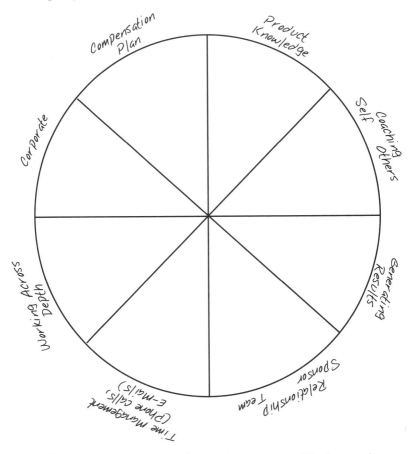

"There are three types of people in the world: those who make things happen, those who watch things happen, and those who wonder what happened!"

~ Author Unknown ~

Let's talk for a minute about balance. My background is Nutrition based in Traditional Chinese Medicine and balance figures prominently in this modality. According to Traditional Chinese Medicine, if the body receives nourishing whole foods, it has the innate power to always seek balance, order and health. When one of the areas is weak, all of the other aspects have to work harder to compensate. The entire health of the body is compromised.

> "If you have always done what you always do, you will always get the same results."
>
> ~ Anonymous ~

In my life I have learned there is an ebb and flow to life and sometimes we have to go out of balance to gain balance. Does your life have balance? When you connect the dots on the Wheel of Life or the Business Wheel or the Balance Model of my network marketing organization, is it a smooth circle? Or do the points spike up and down between sections? Are there areas fulfilled to the brim and other areas barely filled or empty? Is the fullness in your life by conscious choice?

Sometimes we have to work 24-7 just to fit everything into the day. I invite you to keep the big picture in mind and know what's driving you. Right now, get conscious about your life. Ask yourself: If I create abundance but have no life – what is the point? Ask yourself: Am I duplicatable? Ask yourself: Is what I am doing coming from a place of the heart and empowering the people around me, or from a place of control contributing to expanding my own ego? Make a conscious choice now to live fully from your heart in the spirit of service to others.

> "If you wish to find, you must search. Rarely does a good idea interrupt you."
>
> ~ Jim Rohn ~

Dreams & Goals

"A goal is created three times. First as a mental picture. Second, written down to add clarity and dimension. And third, when you take action towards its achievement."

~ from Goals by Gary Ryan Blair ~

Now let's play! Get a notebook or BIG piece of blank paper and get ready to write...capture *in writing* what flows in response to the following questions: When you daydream, what do you see yourself doing? What does your heart long for? What do you desire? What would you love to do? What would you love to accomplish? What would you do if you were guaranteed success? Where could you go if you could go anywhere in the world? Who would you go there with? What clothes would you wear? What food would you eat? What is most important to you in your life right now? What would you keep in your life? What would you let go? Who would you meet if you could meet anyone in the world? Why? These are just a few questions to ask yourself to start thinking . . .

Now write.

Now read the questions again and write some more. Do it from a place of excitement . . . sit up, pull your shoulders back, put a smile on your face and pretend you're a little kid and it's Christmas.

Now you have a stream-of-consciousness list, read over it and write a list of dreams, desires, toys, homes, money, vacations, clothes, contributions . . . what you choose to have in your lifetime . . . I invite you to really use your imagination and write a list of at least 100 or more. Remember, you're a child again, it's Christmas and anything is possible . . .

For me, when I first wrote my goals down on paper, I was really stretched to even come up with anything! My husband and I were in a time-management course and we wrote what we thought were some pretty outrageous things. And I have to tell you, within the first 10 years of our married life we accomplished everything we wrote.

Now get a fresh page . . . and imagine I am a genie and have waved a magic wand. You are already a very successful leader in your company. Right now, what would be new and different in your life . . . (write it down starting with "I am . . . " or "I have . . . ") Now it's 5 years from now and you have diamonds in your organization. Now what's new and different in your life . . . (write it down starting with "I am . . . " or "I have . . . ") Now it's 10 years from now . . . now what's new and different in your life . . .(write it down starting with "I am . . ." or "I have . . .") Now it's 15 years from now . . . now what's new and different in your life . . .(write it down starting with "I am . . ." or "I have . . .")

Goal setting creates a compelling future and the person it will take to achieve all you choose is you. Consider an airplane. What factors get it from the airport where it takes off to the airport where it lands? Flight plan, pilot and specifications…when a plane takes off on auto-pilot, it has a set course and corrects itself right before it lands. Think about taking off without having any navigational instruments on a plane. Over distance, being off by two degrees would result in a much different destination than the one you may have intended! Goals are a concrete way to self-correct and land in the correct place.

Now let's make a slight turn . . . get out your bottle of gratitude essential oil and sniff . . .

"Gratitude is a miracle-working attitude."

~ Anonymous ~

Wake up. Wake up to the quality of your life. Wake up every morning filled with such a profound gratitude for the abundance in your life, it brings tears of joy to your eyes. Sound good? Can you imagine your gratitude? Can you feel your thankfulness? What can you find in your life to be grateful about?

Now get your notebook or BIG piece of paper.

1. Make a list of everything you have to be thankful for in your life.
2. Make a list of achievements you have accomplished in this area of your life.
3. Choose 5 items from your dream-stream to make into your top 1-year goals.
Additional step: Write 1, 3, 5, 10 or 20 years next to each goal and how long it will take you to achieve them.
4. Write down what kind of person it will take to achieve all you have chosen. Describe the character traits, values, beliefs, virtues you would need to embody.

How to Set a Goal

1. WRITE IT, PUT IT IN WRITING, WRITE IT DOWN!
2. Make it "SMART":
   S = Specific
   M = Measurable
   A = Attainable
   R = Realistic
   T = Time-Bound

Achieving Outcomes

- Positively stated
- Evidence procedure (how measured)
- Congruently desirable
- Self-initiated and maintained
- Appropriately contextualized
- What resources are needed (what strategies, more info)
- Ecological (fits in with the rest of their life)

You can also use the categories on the Wheel of Life and the Business Wheel to make goals for each section. Make your goals big, and specific! Make them so big, if (when) you get them, this would be the most important thing that ever happened to you. State your focus as stepping up your Network Marketing success. Once you are clear where you would like to go, a plan can be formulated to get you to your intended destination.

"Goals serve as a stimulus to life.
They tend to tap the deeper resources
and draw out of life its best."

~ Anonymous ~

Decisions ... By When ... Leverage/Why ... Resources

The Mastery of Decisions!

"Influence: there is no greater power to move people to action; to achieve extraordinary results; to create joy, happiness and fulfillment; and to make a positive difference in the quality of people's lives."

~ Anthony Robbins ~

Decision: to cut off from anything else.

Think about where you are right now reading this book…at home, in the car, at a restaurant or coffee shop…and ask yourself, "What decisions got me here?" Every moment, you make decisions affecting the course of your life. They may be small decisions or major ones, conscious action or "go with the flow." Either way, your decision for action or inaction has placed you in your current location! *Every* decision impacts your life and influences its direction. Now think about where you are in the bigger picture of your life. Each of your decisions brought you to where you are now.

What can be improved in your decision making process? Like any other process, decision making is a skill which needs to be developed. Like a muscle, the way to make your decision making skills stronger is to make more decisions. A successful business builder needs to master the art of making a prompt decision. If it has results other than ones you are happy with, learn from it and make another decision! Fear may arise, uncertainty, feeling overwhelmed; simply acknowledge whatever feelings arise and make a conscious choice to decide now.

Factors for Eliciting Decisions

What are your options? Make a list. (One option is no choice, two options are a dilemma, three or more options are true choice.)

What is your desired end result? Get clear about what you choose and why you choose it. How will you know you achieved your desired outcome? What is your purpose? You need to know with specificity what you are choosing and why.

What are your values and in what priority? Is this congruent with who you think or feel you are and what's important to you? Get clear.

Decide to decide now. Remember there is no "best" time to make a decision. Taking too long to decide can be as detrimental as being too impulsive. All decisions are based on probability.

Write your decision on paper. "A blunt pencil is better than a sharp memory."

Question: *There are five eagles sitting on a tree limb. Three of the eagles decide to fly off. How many eagles are left sitting on the tree limb?*

If you answered two, reconsider. Making a decision to fly off is just a decision until there is action to actually fly off! Answer: Five eagles are still sitting on a tree limb.

"A six word formula for success: Think things through, then follow through!"

~ Anonymous ~

You become successful the moment you start moving towards a worthwhile goal. How many people do you know who continually make a decision to build a business, and the next time you talk to them, are still exactly where they were when they made the decision?

In order to extract change, every decision has to have action behind it. Now cut off every other possibility distracting you from your outcome. Now commit to tap into the deeper resources of taking effective action. Decisions serve as a stimulus.

Once a decision has been made using the factors for eliciting decisions mentioned earlier, the next stage is to commit to action, and schedule those actions…make a plan…

The founder of humanistic psychology, Abraham Maslow, presented four levels to learning:

1. Unconscious Incompetence (you don't know what you don't know)
2. Conscious Incompetence (you know you don't know something)
3. Conscious Competence (you learn to do something but it takes your full concentration)
4. Unconscious Competence (you can do something without having to think about it anymore. You're a master!)

As you are building your business and creating rapport with people, you will go through these four stages of learning. You are building a skill level until you get to the place where it's just who you are and you can do it without thinking about it anymore!

The Driving Forces of Human Behavior!

"To understand the heart and mind of a person,
look not at what he has already achieved,
but at what he aspires to."

~ Kahlil Gibran ~

P ay very close attention—this is the most important tool you can utilize to motivate people. When you really assess from a place of the heart what drives people, what needs they are attempting to fill and seek to lovingly fill those needs, something profound happens. You tap into the largest source of power in existence . . . power from the heart.

Human beings, regardless of race or gender, all have a certain force driving them and shaping their actions and behaviors. This information changed my life when I first heard it touched on by Anthony Robbins in 2001. Tapping into this driving force is the single greatest tool I can give you to create successful relationships with people and to motivate them. When you can naturally understand what's going on with a person, you can connect with them in a way nothing else can give you. This driving force is what can push people to create charities or million-dollar industries on the positive side, or on the negative side, to commit gruesome crimes.

Every person has deep within them two primary fears as well as seven emotional/psychological needs. Their two primary fears are they will not be loved or they are not enough. Their seven emotional/psychological needs are security/ certainty, variety/creativity, recognition/significance, connection/love, personal growth/development, contribution and a compelling future.

Everyone is actively dominant with two of the seven emotional/psychological needs. Most people are unaware this very powerful driving force is at work. Most people are unconsciously attempting to fill these needs and because one or more of them are unfulfilled, they will have an underlying restlessness, irritability or tenseness without knowing why. This happens whenever one or more of these seven emotional/psychological needs go unfulfilled.

On the other side, whenever three or more of these needs are met at a high level at the same time, what is essentially an addiction occurs. The addiction response can be positive, neutral or negative, depending on the person and circumstances. Knowing what emotional/psychological needs are driving a person provides the opportunity to creatively fulfill those needs on a conscious level.

The 7 Emotional / Psychological Needs

Security/Certainty = Survival; control; consistency.
It's the reason people will rent or buy a movie and watch it multiple times—they like the feeling it gives them or knowing the ending.

Variety/Creativity = Diversity; surprise; challenge; excitement; originality of thought or action.
It's the reason you don't eat the same thing for breakfast, lunch and dinner day after day.

Recognition/Significance = Acknowledgement; praise; sense of being needed; sense of purpose; feeling important; uniqueness.
Everyone needs to feel important to someone or something.

Connection/Love = Associating with others; benevolent affection; bonding; sharing; intimacy; relationship; uniting.

Everyone needs to feel connected to an organization, club, church, etc., loved by a person or an animal.

Personal Growth/Development = Increase; generate or acquire; to bring out the possibilities of; bring to a more advanced, effective or usable state.

All things are either growing or dying.

Contribution/Legacy = Giving; provide, supply or accomplish.

After you have everything, then what? You have to give back.

A Compelling Future = Driving course of action.

Something to live for, to give your life purpose.

"There are two things people want more than
sex and money. Recognition and praise."

~ Mary Kay Ash ~

Do You Know Your Why

When I discovered my why for building my network marketing business, it compelled me from my core with passion. I have heard that your why is more important than the how. And I discovered in my research that what I thought was my why was actually not the core of what was driving me daily to keep building after 30 years in the industry with the highest rank and a 7 figure income. As a Psychoneurologist, I am trained in my education to look for the core or reasons behind our behaviors. I discovered that there are 9 core Whys. We will resonate with all, but only one will put smile on our face and drive us through the ups and downs of life. The remaining 8 will be how we achieve the one that resonates in our core. In resources, you will find recommended books and an assessment for finding your why.

"He who has a why to live can bear almost any how."

~ Friedrich Nietzsche ~

The 9 Whys:

1. To contribute to greater cause, make a difference or add value

2. To build trust or create relationships based on trust

3. To make sense out of things, especially if complex or complicate

4. To find a better way

5. To do things right or the right way

6. To think differently and challenge the status quo

7. To master things, or seek knowledge

8. To clarify, create clarity and understanding

9. To simplify

Network Marketing is all about people and relationships. I will say it again…Network Marketing is all about people and relationships. People will buy from you after they have established a relationship with you and they are certain you care about them. They must have certainty you really have their best interest at heart. It is human nature to always move away from pain or towards pleasure. People have to feel certain their pain will go away or pleasure will return. They must know what it is worth to them, what is in it for them, if it will give them what they need and if you can prove it. They also need to be certain they need it NOW! They must feel security around what other people will think or how other people will respond. In fact, when I find out someone is interested in the business and they are married, I ask to meet with the spouse/significant other also. Remember, we are building long-term relationships, so start out with both parts of the team!

Create a space for their needs to be fulfilled in a positive manner. The tool of identifying a person's emotional/psychological needs will enhance your relationship and forge long-lasting bonds. Another way to understand their unique needs and really communicate with them in a heart-felt manner is to find out their love language. The book "The Five Love Languages: How to Express Heartfelt Commitment to Your Mate" by Gary Chapman includes a personal assessment tool. (Note: although it is written for husband and wife, I use this tool for any significant others, including a business partner or friend.) It is available at www.fivelovelanguages.com.

In fact, take a step beyond the average and really look at where your breakdowns in relationship occur. Almost all breakdowns in business will come down to some unmet need or "talking" in a language the other person can't understand. What can you do to raise your level of understanding about how the people you are in relationships with communicate their needs and desires and how can you supply them? Use these tools!

The Building Block of Relationship: Rapport!

"The most important single ingredient in the formula of success is knowing how to get along with people."

~ Theodore Roosevelt ~

R epetition is the mother of skill, so I will repeat – building a successful network marketing business is really building successful relationships. I would like to emphasize here, if you use these techniques coming from your head or ego instead of your heart, people will feel manipulated instead of appreciated. There is a level of skill required to establish connection with people and an even higher skill level to establish it in a harmonious or compassionate manner so the other person feels appreciated, understood and respected. The saying goes, the more you are like someone, the more they will like you. This higher level skill goes a step beyond simple liking, and actually *creates the need for responsiveness*. This is called rapport.

In order to master this skill of connecting with people it is important to lay aside any preconceived judgments you might have about the other person, their life, who they are and what they are capable of doing or not doing. As children we are taught judgment as a tool to survive – touching a hot stove will burn us, crossing the street without looking might get us killed, those sorts of things. It is part of our life training to live to adulthood. As we get older, we expand those judgments to include people we will or will not associate with, what we will wear or not wear, where we will live or not live. We go into a sort of trance and do the same things every day, with the same sorts of people, in the same way, at the same time, etc. And we are safe. We are on auto-pilot. So I invite you to set aside your automatic internal judgment of what you think or feel about how someone else looks, their clothes, hair, or skin color, what you think or feel about what they drive, where they might live, how much money or education they might have…set aside anything you might be hallucinating about them in order to connect from your heart. This is vitally important because the moment you judge someone, you lose the ability to influence them. Never assume anything about what the other person thinks, feels, hears, sees, knows, or understands. Never assume anything!

> "There is nothing either good or bad,
> but thinking makes it so."
>
> ~ William Shakespeare ~

The following is an e-mail grapevine story which may or may not be true. It is something to think about…

> "A lady in a faded gingham dress and her husband, dressed in a homespun threadbare suit, stepped off the train in Boston. They walked timidly without an appointment into the President of Harvard's outer office. The secretary could tell in a moment that such backwoods country folks had no business at Harvard and probably did not even deserve to be in Cambridge. She frowned.
> "We choose to see the President," the man said softly.
> "He'll be busy all day," the secretary snapped.
> "We'll wait," the lady replied.

For hours the secretary ignored them, hoping the couple would finally become discouraged and go away. They didn't. The secretary grew frustrated and finally decided to disturb the President, even though it was a chore she always regretted to do. "Maybe if they just see you for a few minutes, they'll leave," she told him. He sighed in exasperation and nodded. Someone of his importance obviously didn't have the time to spend with them, but he detested gingham and homespun suits cluttering his office.

The President, stern-faced with dignity, strutted toward the couple.

The lady told him, "We had a son that attended Harvard for one year. He loved Harvard, and was very happy here. But a year ago, he was accidentally killed. My husband and I would like to erect a memorial to him somewhere on campus."

The president wasn't touched, he was shocked. "Madam," he said gruffly, "We can't put up a statue for every person who attended Harvard and died. If we did, this place would look like a cemetery."

"Oh no" the lady explained quickly, "We don't choose to erect a statue. We thought we would give a building to Harvard."

The President rolled his eyes. He glanced at the gingham dress and homespun suit, then exclaimed, "A building!! Do you have any earthly idea how much a building costs? We have over seven and a half million dollars in the physical plans at Harvard!!"

For a moment the lady was silent. The President was pleased. He could get rid of them now. The lady turned to her husband. She said quietly, "Is that all it costs to start a university? Why don't we just start our own?" Her husband nodded.

The President's face wilted in confusion and

bewilderment. Mr. and Mrs. Leland Stanford walked away, traveling to Palo Alto, CA where they established the university that bears their name…a memorial to a son that Harvard no longer cared about."

Something to think about!...

⌬

It is also important to enter the other person's "world." No two people experience life exactly the same way. Each person lives according to their own version of reality… nothing in life has meaning except the meaning you give it. Each person operates their life from their own perspective of reality. To really understand a person, you must be able to perceive the world from *their* point of view, from their experiences and preferences. Learn to set aside your personal filters to understand the other person's model of the world. Forget about yourself, focus on the other person. Learn to connect from their world.

The quality of our lives is the quality of our communications. People are constantly communicating in their own style. The saying goes, "The more you are like someone, the more you are liked." Most people believe the words they speak are the highest importance in communication. Studies show words are the smallest component of communication, comprising only 7 percent. What people really "hear" first is what they "see" in the physiology of the other person! 55 percent of communication is projected from the physiology of the other person, followed by 38 percent interpreted from the tone used. Become aware of the communication beyond the words in order to establish heart-felt connection.

Really get the importance of this information! How much does it matter how carefully you formulate the words in your sentence if the other person is put off by the tone you are using to speak to them, and/or the way your body is situated as you say it? It matters 93 percent, because you may have alienated them or connected with them, depending on how you were communicating! In order to create rapport, step into someone's world in a variety of ways.

Verbal Language Pattern:
o Words: Predicates, Key words, Common experiences and associations
o Tonality: Tone (pitch), Tempo – speed fast slow moderate, Timbre/quality, Volume/loudness or softness
External Behavior:
o Physiology: Posture, Gesture, Facial expression and blinking, Breathing, Eyes

One way to connect with someone is "matching and mirroring," a technique developed by Dr. Milton Erickson, in which you match how they express themselves using the above keys. Think of a fast-speaking New Yorker…they might find frustrating someone speaking in a "slow Southern drawl" and connect with another "fast-talker!" Or a quiet speaker might avoid a loud speaker! If the fast speaker would slow down the rate of speech, the slower speaker would connect more readily; if the volume of the other speaker is made louder or softer, there would also be more rapport.

Personology is another technique to build rapport. It is a hands-on teaching I highly recommend. I credit Naomi Tickle, whose book is listed in the resource section.

Another way is to "match" their sensory system. A person's words reflect what sensory system they use, whether it is predominantly Visual, Auditory, or Kinesthetic. Listen for specific predicates in a person's speech pattern, and identify which category it falls into. This will tell you what words and phrases to use to most effectively connect and raise responsiveness.

An example of this from my own life: My husband Jim is kinesthetic; I am auditory-visual. For years in our conversations I would talk to him and he just wouldn't get what I was telling him. Someone else would tell him the exact same thing, and he would get it. I would say, "Do you see…" Finally I realized the reason he would get it with them! They would say, "Do you feel…" Now I say, "Do you feel…" and touch him, and he gets it! Sincerely using words from a person's sensory style will help them really get what you are saying with grace and ease.

The following are specifically constructed examples using words which will connect with visual, auditory or kinesthetic based people. Here, Donald Clair brilliantly created these three solid examples for you to tap into:

Business 1 – Visual
PICTURE this: a business nothing short of IL-LUMINATING excellence. LOOK at how the business is directed towards individuals who may truly have limited time to FOCUS their attention towards it. Yet, the time invested creates such abundance each moment adds value towards the ultimate VISION one has created. It's like being able to place the exact amount of SUNSHINE into the SHADOWS of the business world and create your destiny.

Business 2 – Auditory
Have you ever HEARD of a business opportunity beckoning you? As this business opportunity CALLS to you, it QUIETLY allows a place to make your own STATEMENT about which direction YOU TELL yourself you need to go. As you explored the inner mechanism of the business, it TOLD you it functions like a well-TUNED engine. The incentive plan simply SPEAKS volumes about what the long-term potentials are in store for you. It has a business feature CALLED quality reputation and when you HEARD about this point you knew you could be comfortable TALKING to others about this opportunity.

Business 3 – Kinesthetic

How would it FEEL to GRASP HOLD of a business opportunity giving you a FIRM place to STAND as you BUILT your future? Have you ever considered a business opportunity that TOUCHES your very core and allows you the position to grow and expand? A business opportunity providing you tools to open the fields ahead as you WALK and enjoy being a part of a company center based on a history of quality and excellence. When one chooses this business opportunity it will finally FEEL like "this is where I belong."

A few more examples:

VISUAL: "If I could REVEAL to you a CLEAR way in which you could (their value or benefit), you would LOOK at it, right? If this LOOKS good to you, we will go ahead and FOCUS on getting started."

AUDITORY: "If I could DESCRIBE a way in which you could (their value or benefit), you would LISTEN, right? If this SOUNDS good to you, we will go ahead and DISCUSS getting started."

KINESTHETIC: "If I could HAND you a CONCRETE way in which you could (their benefit or value), you would FEEL it out, right? If this FEELS good to you, we will go ahead and HANDLE getting started."

This is something to really get excited about! Building rapport and entering a person's world through sensory techniques is truly profound and an advanced skill level. The average person hasn't even heard of these tools let alone taken steps to learn them and apply them. I invite you to really play with V.A.K. and discover the results for yourself! Print out the V.A.K. sensory word list and put it by the phone. Really listen as they speak to get a feel for their style. See what words appear in your conversation from each list. Make notes so it becomes natural to you. Then talk to them in their style.

This is a phenomenal tool for gaining people's interest. If a person is visual and you have them listen to a CD, there is a much smaller likelihood they will be interested than if you give them a DVD to watch. If the person is kinesthetic and you are only talking, putting something in their hands they can touch will have better results. Giving an auditory person material to read is less effective than talking to them. Know how to support people with material in their sensory style and you will have awesome results!

The following is a list of words for each sensory style: Visual, Auditory, Kinesthetic and comprises what we call the "VAK list."

VISUAL:

SEE
Appear
Black & White
Blank
Bright
Clarify
Clear
Colorful (using colors)
Crystal
Dark
Dawn
Dull
Envision
Focused
Foggy

Fuzzy
Gleam
Glint
Glossy
Gray
Hazy
Illuminate
Illusion
Imagine
Lighten up
Look
Pale
Peek
Perspective

Picture
Reveal
Scan
Scene
Shadow
Shiny
Show
Sparkle
Staring
Tint
Vague
View
Vivid
Vision

AUDITORY:

HEAR
Banging around
Be all ears
Be heard
Bells
Can't hear myself
Clear as a bell
Clicks
Deaf
Describe
Dissonance
Ears
Harmony
Inquire
Listen

Loud
Mellifluous
Music
Noise
On that note
Orchestrate
Piercing
Piped
Quiet
Question
Rattling
Resonate
Rings
Roared
Rumble

Say
Silence
Sound (using sounds)
Speaks
State
Static
Talk
Tell
Tone
Tongue
Trickle
Tune
Unhearing
Vibration

KINESTHETIC:

FEEL
Absorb
Beat
Blown away
Catch on
Cold
Comfortable
Concrete
Dry
Firm
Flush
Fragmented
Grasp, grip
Hand
Hard

Hit
Hold
Lean
Lighter
Make contact
Moving/moves
Nail down
Penetrate
Pressure
Push
Rough
Scrape
Shake
Shoulder
Slip through

Smooth
Solid
Stir
Tap into
Throw
Tip-toe
Toss
Touch
Tread
Tremble
Unfeeling
Walk
Warm
Weight

Compensation

"NETWORK MARKETING IS THE FASTEST
GROWING HOME-BASED BUSINESS
OPPORTUNITY IN THE WORLD!"

~ Anonymous ~

I have been involved in the network marketing business since the early eighties. The companies I have been associated with were all product-oriented. There were times when I did not even understand the compensation plans! And I have seen a lot of them...... Personally, I achieved great success with the strategy my products are *people*. For me this is Relationship marketing. "Word of Mouth" product endorsement is the most powerful marketing paradigm today! My mentor taught me to sponsor and build wide to create income and to teach my organization to duplicate what I'm doing creating depth.

There are companies centered around health products. We are attracting a lot of sick people and people who are searching for alternative health solutions. With a health product company, I am now looking for investors who will invest in their health and their financial future.

If you focus on products in your business you will attract product users; if you also focus your attention on the business side, you will attract business builders.

"Network marketing - making a living
while making a difference."

~Marcella Vonn Harting ~

In Network Marketing the "big" money is made from creating leaders building the business. Have you ever heard of the 80/20 Principle? This applies to our business.....80 percent of your organization will be product users; be grateful, the 20 percent who step up for the business will produce more than all the 80 percent!

"It's not lonely at the top; it's
crowded at the bottom!!!"

~ Anonymous ~

The Price of the Promise

The following was sent to me by a good friend, I feel there is some excellent wisdom here for building a successful networking business.

Mark Yarnell, minister in a small town in Texas, was headed for bankruptcy and just about to lose his car and home. He looked for a way out and discovered network marketing. Luckily, he had a wise sponsor.

The sponsor gave Mark "the promise": this business can set you free financially in one to three years. But he also gave him the price. To succeed, you will have to face and conquer 4 major enemies. Mark said, "It's a deal."

He then invited 200 friends over to his house to watch a video. 80 said "No, not interested."

Mark had encountered Enemy # 1: Rejection.

He thought, "No problem. My sponsor warned me about that. I've got 120 people still coming over." Guess what? 50 didn't show up.

He had just met Enemy #2: Deception

Mark thought, "No proplem. My sponsor

warned me about that. I've got 70 people who watched the tape." Guess what? 57 said, "Not interested."

He had just encountered Enemy #3: Apathy.

Undaunted, Mark thought, "No problem. 13 people signed up." Guess what? 12 of them dropped out of the business shortly thereafter.

Enemy #4: Attrition had left Mark with just one serious associate. To this day, that single distributor earns Mark over $50,000 per month.

You may have heard of Bill Britt, one of the most successful distributors in Amway. Some years ago, 20/20 did a feature story on Amway. They spent 19 minutes interviewing whiners and complainers—several distributors who had failed—and showed the garages full of products they couldn't sell. During the last minute of the show, Mr. Britt was interviewed in front of his palatial home. He was asked, "Mr. Britt, this business has obviously worked for you. What's your secret?"

He replied, "There is no secret. I simply showed the plan to 1200 people. 900 said, 'no' and only 300 signed up. Out of those 300, only 85 did anything at all. Out of those 85 only 35 were serious, and out of those 35, 11 made me a millionaire." Like Mark Yarnell, Bill worked through the numbers.

Jason Boreyko, now president of New Vision, told this story recently. When he was a distributor in Matol, he signed up 50 people. He heard a lot of "no's" on the way to those 50. Jason took one man who he knew would be terrific in the business to lunch, told him about the business and the man said, "No." Then Jason took the man to lunch again the next month and told him the updates. Once again the man said, "No." Jason sent him some more information and took him to lunch again the next month. And again the man said "No." That went on for six months. The seventh month, something had changed for the man, and he said, "Yes." That man made Jason over one million dollars. Jason also worked through his numbers.

According to Richard Poe in "Wave Three," while starting Amway, Rich De Vos and Jay Van Andel, America's eleventh richest people, recruited 500 people. 495 dropped out. The five that didn't quit built Amway. All $7 billion of Amway's business was built under those 5 people. Jay and Rich had to work through their numbers. There are many similar stories.

Jett, the top money earner in Mannatech, signed up 27 people in his first month. One might think that he is especially talented at sponsoring. Actually, Jett will be the first to tell you that he is not talented at all. In fact he feels that he did very poorly. To recruit those 27, Jett talked to 2000 people that first month. And of the 27 the only one who did anything significant with the business was Ray Gebauer, who has more than half of Mannatech in his downline. Jett's word to you is that the numbers never lie. Pick your goal and then get into massive action. If you talk to enough people, you will make it.

Here's the lesson: your success is directly related to the degree to which you are willing to work to find others like yourself who are committed to succeed. Mark Yarnell's odds were 1 out of 50. (Jett's were really 1 out of 2000.) Would you be willing to go through 200 people to find the 1 who will make you $50,000 a month? Or go through 200 people to become a millionaire? Or hear uncounted "no's" to sign up 50 people to find a million dollar person? I hope you will…it's easier when you know the odds up front.

But here's the catch: you have your own set of odds and you won't know what they are until after you've succeeded. So if you've gone through 50 or 100 people and you haven't found 1 serious person yet, you can either give up and assume the business doesn't work or recognize that you are working though your own numbers.

Are you willing to find out your own set of

odds? That means you must pay the price for freedom. Remember, the numbers never fail you. Despite where you are in your skill level, your success is assured if you talk to enough people. And as your skill improves, so will your odds…there is no such thing as luck in this industry. Winning big is a matter of being willing to pay the price. Are you? Your future is in your hands. The choices which you make today will determine the course of your entire future.

May you have a successful future in all aspects of your life!

⤙⫚⤚

I really choose for you to get this: success in this business is equal to your willingness to connect with people. From my heart, in the big picture of this business, it comes down to numbers of people! And you can know only a handful of people and still be really successful in this business! Because the people you know, know other people, who know other people, who know other people…get it?! And when you connect with people from a place of real sincerity and heart, they are willing to bridge you with their friends. When you feel so passionate about other people and their dreams being fulfilled and their heart's desires being met, miracles happen!

Now I really choose for you to get this: just like in the story of "The Promise," you will have to work through your numbers and overcome rejection, deception, apathy and attrition to find those people who will really be part of your success. This is why it is so important to use every aspect of this book for your success. Know your purpose in sharing this opportunity with others so you can keep moving forward and "working through" your numbers! Find your personal leverage so you know how to motivate yourself when you choose to slow down or stay down!

Network Marketing is based on a calendar month. Every month we start all over and we get paid for the last month. In creating a solid base, I look for ways to make sure everything is set up to flow as smoothly as possible. Keep any possible challenges from occurring: like a credit card not getting processed or some system glitch, etc.…If the check you are receiving is paying a mortgage or car payment, let's make sure you have done your part to dot all your i's and cross all your t's so you receive the check.

As a basic fundamental business strategy this is imperative. If you are as unwise as to NOT be on auto-ship and put off placing your order until the last few days of the month, if ANY "glitch" occurs in the system, you could miss your whole check! Think about it! Or if it should happen you die suddenly, your family might lose your entire check and it would roll up to your up-line! Is that your highest choice? I am advising you…put your minimum $100.00 PV auto-ship to ship by the 21st or better yet, the 14th.

As another business strategy, consider what you recommend to others when they are setting up their orders. Another beautiful aspect of many company's products is they are "consumable" – meaning they get used up and need to be replaced! Certain products will take longer to use than others.

Network Marketing really is a credible business, so shift into treating it like one! Did you know your business can be sold, gifted or willed to someone? (As long as it is done in accordance with the requirements of the policies and procedures.) This is a business, use business strategies! I have listed some books in the resource section I advise you to read!

In the industry of Network Marketing and MLM, no matter what the company or the product, there is a magic number…which is $300.00. If I can get you to receive a check of around $300.00 within 90 days of the day you signed up, the statistics show you will stay with the company. You may not actively pursue a business; you will remain a product user.

I came across the diagram "The Power of Community" many years ago. It is another visual reminder of how the numbers never lie! These numbers represent people and people are our business…if you don't talk to them, someone else will!!! *SOMETHING TO THINK ABOUT!*

THE POWER OF COMMUNITY

It is amazing to realize what would happen if today you signed up one new person and tomorrow those two each signed up one new person and the following day they each signed up one new person who each signed up one new person….

This is what the math would look like:

Day:	Number of people:
1	1
2	2
3	4
4	8
5	16
6	32
7	64
8	128
9	256
10	512
11	1,024
12	2,048
13	4,096
14	8,192
15	16,384
16	32,768
17	65,536
18	131,072
19	262,144
20	524,288
21	1,048,576
22	2,097,152
23	4,194,304
24	8,388,608
25	16,777,216
26	23,554,432
27	47,108,864
28	94,217,728
29	188,435,456
30	376,870,902

What remarkable results from one person simply sharing with another person!!!

Leadership

The success of a leader is defined by their ability to influence. Think about it! If you're out walking and you turn around and no one is behind you, you're not a leader, you're just out on a walk! If you're walking along and talk to someone and they start walking with you, then you're a leader!

The most effective way to lead is by leading others to success. The structure of Network Marketing is win-win: the more successful you become, the more successful I become. People are willing to follow people who have a win-win philosophy. Find someone's passion and light their fire...people continually have someone lighting a fire under them; a true leader will ignite a person's internal passion.

Leadership principles and skills can be learned. Link leadership principles and skills with your heart-felt desires and you have the formula for becoming a successful leader.

I am in the position I am in life and in this company because of all of you. I am profoundly grateful and blessed every day. Thank you, God bless you, Marcella Vonn Harting

Resources

www.MarcellaVonnHarting.com

Business cards/stationary:
www.Alexanders.com
www.VistaPrint.com

Love Languages Assessment:
www.fivelovelanguages.com
(click on link for '30 Second Assessment')

Guerrilla Marketing for Network Marketers:
www.gmmlm.com

Training Tapes and CDs:
www.DaniJohnson.com or call 1-866-760-8255
www.GrowthPro.com or call 1-205-871-2998
www.YLWebsite.com
www.NetworkingTimes.com or call 1-866-343-4005 or Int'l
818-727-2000

Sound Concepts:
www.crowndiamondtools.soundconcepts.com
www.essentialproductinfo.soundconcepts.com
or call 1-800-524-4195

LSP Life Science Publishers
1216 South 1580 West, suite A
Orem, Utah 84058
800-336-6308
www.lifesciencepublishers.com

Emotional Release Technology
The Philosopher's Stone
by Jan Adams 828-631-3903
www.myphilosopherstone.com

Mastery Systems
352 Depot St, Suite 210
Asheville NC 28801
828-258-2220,   email: IAM@masterysystems.com
www.masterysystems.com

American Botanical Council
www.herbalgram.org
800-373-7105 or 512-926-4900

Alexander's Print Advantage
printware@alexanders.com

Scott Burnett, Esq.
www.BurnettandAssociates.com
scott@BurnettandAssociates.com
877-836-9691
Business & Tax Education Specialists
Business education for the sole proprietor, corporation or LLC
business owner. *The more you know, the less you will owe.*

TAX INFORMATION RESOURCE

www.TheBusinessOwnersBootCamp.com
Online video, webinar and educational website for business law
and business and personal taxation.

TAX BOOKS:

- *Lower Your Taxes,* by Sandy (Sanford) Botkin, CPA, McGraw Hill Publication © 2003; ISBN: 0-07-140807-X, www.books.mcgraw-hill.com
- *Small Time Operator: How to Start Your Own Business, Keep Your Books, Pay Your Taxes, and Stay Out of Trouble!,* by Bernard B. Kamoroff, CPA; Bell Springs Publishing; ISBN: 0917510259
- *Tax Strategies for Business Professionals,* by Sandy (Sanford) Botkin, CPA; TRI Publication © 1989-2002; Tax Reduction Institute 13200 Executive Park Terrace, Germantown, Maryland 20874, 1-800-874-

0829, FAX 1-301-972-0819, www.taxreductioninstitute.com
- *It's How Much You KEEP That Counts! Not How Much You Make*, by Ronald R. Mueller; Publisher: Fidlar Doubleday ©2000; ISBN: 0-9707528-0-2

Tax Savings for a Home Based Business
https://taxbot.com/z/9n/

To qualify for tax deductions, you must...
1. Demonstrate that you intend to make a profit.
2. Work your business on a regular and consistent basis.
3. Run your small business like any other 'real' business.
4. Record all of your business expenses, income and activity.

A FEW BOOKS EVERYONE SHOULD READ

BUSINESS BOOKS:

1. *Guerrilla Multilevel Marketing,* by Jay Conrad Levinson, James Dillehay & Marcella Vonn Harting
2. *Start With Why*, by Simon Sinek
3. *The Why Engine*, by Ridgely Goldsborough, Esq.
4. *Think and Grow Rich*, by Napoleon Hill
5. *How to Win Friends and Influence People*, by Dale Carnegie
6. *The Richest Man in Babylon*, by George S. Clason
7. *The Greatest Networker*, by John Milton Fogg
8. *Man's Search for Meaning*, by Viktor E. Frankl
9. *See You at the Top*, by Zig Ziglar
10. *Greatest Salesman that Ever Lived*, by Og Mandino
11. *Being The Best You Can Be in MLM*, by John Kalench
12. *Twelve Pillars*, by Jim Rohn & Chris Widener

13. *The Traveler's Gift*, by Andy Andrews
14. *You Can Read A Face Like A Book*, by Naomi Tickle
15. *Amazing Face Reading*, by Mac Fuller, J.D.
16. *The Five Love Languages*, by Gary Chapman
17. *The Secret*, by Rhonda Byrne
18. *Unlimited Power*, by Anthony Robbins
19. *Introducing NLP*, by Joseph O'Connor & John Seymour
20. *The Unfair Advantage; Sell with NLP*, by Duane Lakin, PhD

HEALTH BOOKS:

1. *Feelings Buried Alive Never Die*, by Karol Truman
2. *You Can Heal Your Life*, by Louise Hay
3. *Molecules of Emotion*, by Candace B. Pert, PhD
4. *Yes, No, Maybe Chronobiotic Nutrition*, by Marcella Vonn Harting & Atom Bergstrom

"Yes No Maybe"
Chronobiotic Nutrition
by Marcella Vonn Harting, PhD

Chronobiotic™ Nutrition is about being on time in time all the time. It celebrates eating foods at precise times of day for specific health results. When this system of eating is followed, the benefits are optimum digestion, nutritional efficiency, high-level wellness, and robust vitality.

The human body would be in a state of total nutrient lockup without the synchronization of all phyiological transportation of fluids and solids. The antidote to nutritional gridlock is a time-controlled eating protocol like Chronobiotics™. Attending to the cellular "terrain" of the body is useless without attending to the terrain's time-specific traffic laws.

"This book has identified the hidden key of chronobiotics, which was previously unrecognized and which accelerates healing and good health. The book clearly defines the unique factor of time as it relates to the human body and the rhythm of the planet earth. This phenomenon may truly be the hidden link. It is a must read for anyone who would choose a healthy lifestyle."

~ Terry Shepherd Friedmann, M.D., A.B.H.M. ~
One of 25 pioneers in Holistic Medicine

$18, Published by: Yes No Maybe Publishing
Order From
www.MarcellaVonnHarting.com

Highest Potential Academy

Hands-On Experiential Training to Take Your Life & Business to the Level you Envision with Dr. Marcella Vonn Harting

Gain the advanced strategies, skills, and techniques that have built some of the largest organizations in the world. The faculty of Highest Potential Academy has brought together the most in-depth training on advanced technique and skills in building your business. The topics and growth experienced over these few days will not only change your business, but your relationships with your family, friends, and even yourself!

A number of attendees from the first year's event reported their organization quickly ranked higher. They saw greater satisfaction in their lives and relationships. Prior attendees have pointed to the Highest Potential Academy as a paradigm shift in their lives. This is more than a "let's get together and feel good" this is a "let's get together and grow in areas that you never conceived were previously possible."

www.HighestPotentialAcademy.com
or 1-480-443-3224

Don't Miss Out on Your Next Step in Network Marketing Training

Co-authored by Dr. Marcella Vonn Harting, Ph.D.
Marcella Vonn Harting is a Master
Network Marketer and Trainer.

Guerrilla Multilevel Marketing brings you proven advantages from the best-selling marketing series of all time to Network Marketing. Over 21,000,000 Guerrilla books have sold in 41 languages.

Guerrilla Multilevel Marketing delivers 100 tactics to help you increase your network marketing product sales and help you activate and retain more distributors in your downline.

√ Create a personalized blueprint for success with a 6-sentence marketing plan

√ Eliminate fear of the unknown. The guerrilla system puts you in control of your business

√ Position your products to audiences ignored by others

√ Discover the number one reason people buy anything and how you can supply it

√ Learn 12 easy-to-apply ways to get people to commit

√ Get 14 tactics for growing online

√ Boost your sales using more than 60 excuses for following up with prospects

√ And much, much more

Order Your Copy
visit www.GMMLM.com
(available as paperback or e-book/Kindle)